Published by
Action Transport Theatre Company Ltd,
Whitby Hall,
Stanney Lane,
Ellesmere Port,
Cheshire,
England,
CH65 9AE.
Telephone +44 (0)151 357 2120.
www.actiontransporttheatre.co.uk
info@actiontransporttheatre.co.uk

Action Transport Theatre Company Ltd, the individual writers and theatre-makers hereby assert and give notice of their right under section 77 of the UK Copyright, Designs and Patented Act 1988 to be identified as the authors of The Skeleton Key.

Edited by Joe Sumsion,
Artistic Director/Chief Executive,
Action Transport Theatre Company

Publication Project Manager - Jessica Egan,
Promotions & Marketing Manager,
Action Transport Theatre Company

10 9 8 7 6 5 4 3 2 1
ISBN 978-0-9554918-0-1

Design by Sam Hutchinson (re:align:design)
www.realigndesign.com

THE SKELETON KEY

Unlocking the secrets of writing outstanding plays *for* and *by* young people

Published by Action Transport Theatre Company

Edited by Joe Sumsion

This publication has been made possible with the generous support of

The Foyle Foundation
The Granada Foundation
North West Playwrights

YOUR KEY

5

Joe Sumsion - Editor
Artistic Director/Chief Executive
Action Transport Theatre Company

The Skeleton Key offers writers, theatre-makers and teachers an insight into how leading professional theatre-makers practice their craft.

The book focuses on new plays and has three broad sections. Firstly, it asks five leading companies to unpick one of their productions, revealing some of the key steps to how it was written and made. Then Charles Way, one of the UK's leading writers for young people, offers a very personal insight into his process and the challenges he faces as a writer. Finally, the book explores a number of approaches which are being taken to encourage young writers, including a vivid account of one eighteen year old woman's journey to becoming a writer.

These contributions are framed by two pieces: Lyn Gardner's look at a range of approaches to working with writers and John Retallack's reflection on the essence of quality in young people's theatre.

The contributions reveal a thirst amongst young people, companies and writers to work collaboratively. Two key questions emerge in the book: how best can a collaborative process use an individual writer, and where is the space for the individual writer to develop his or her own unique vision?

The Skeleton Key grew out of a three day festival, *The Lockpickers' Ball*, which took place in Liverpool in 2006. Our thanks go to the contributors, supporters and delegates who made that event possible.

THE SKELETON KEY:
INTRODUCTION

Joe Sumsion - Photo by Sylvia Selzer

Lyn Gardner is an experienced theatre critic and vocal supporter of professional theatre for children and young people.

Here she paints a grim picture of traditional new writing theatre. She then goes on to celebrate some of the collaborative approaches which are re-imagining and re-shaping contemporary British theatre.

Earlier this year in the pages of The Guardian, the playwright Colin Teevon - one of a group of playwrights who call themselves the Monsterists and who are attempting to get bigger plays by contemporary writers produced on our main stages - told a story about the director Peter Hall. Apparently Hall was at a dinner party one evening when the lady beside him commented: "What would poor Samuel Beckett's career have been like if *Waiting for Godot* hadn't landed on your desk?" "My dear lady," replied Hall, "imagine what mine would have been like if it hadn't?"

The story is instructive because it demonstrates the power of both the playwright and the director in British theatre, and also the importance of the relationship between the two. A playwright's career really cannot thrive unless she or he is working with the right director who has the foot in the door of a producing house and the ear of the artistic director and who is prepared to champion that playwright's work; similarly a director working in the field of new writing must be associated with the hottest playwright of the moment if her or his career is to thrive. These relationships go on all the time: James Macdonald and Sarah Kane, Max Stafford Clark and Caryl Churchill, Anna Mackmin and Charlotte Jones, Nicolas Hytner and Alan Bennett to name but a few. The playwright who does not have a champion is in danger of being a playwright who quite simply does not have a career.

WRITING AS COLLABORATION- EXPERIMENTS IN FORM

Lyn Gardner - Photo by Maggie Robinson

Clearly these writer/director relationships have often proved fruitful for British theatre over the last century or more, although one also wonders how many other *Waiting for Godots* have been missed over the years for want of a director with the vision to recognize that the script which has landed on his or her desk is a genuinely great one. Nowadays of course if *Waiting For Godot* landed on the desk of the artistic director of one of our new writing theatres it would immediately be put into "development" as part of that theatre's Arts Council funded playwrighting scheme.

Some months – maybe years – later after a series of workshops, one to one sessions with the literary manager and several associates all of whom would insist on putting their finger in the pie, and perhaps a reading, the play may emerge again only for the playwright to be told that after all the tinkering and the many drafts the theatre won't after all be putting the play on.

Playwriting by committee clearly doesn't work. The last great flowering of British playwriting was in the early to mid-1990s with the emergence of a group of writers such as Philip Ridley, Mark Ravenhill, Sarah Kane, Simon Bent and others. This was in an era long before the arrival of playwrighting development schemes - an invention of the TV industry and American academia - on these shores. Without doubt the triumph of these schemes has been to create better access for writers to theatres, but whether it creates better plays is a moot point. The danger is that theatres are now funded in such a way that it suits them to have many writers in development rather than just a few. As a result they may be failing to see the woods for the trees. British playwrighting may not be in crisis, but seasons at new writing theatres from **Soho** to **Royal Court** suggest that it is hardly in tiptop shape.

My feeling is that the energy in British theatre has moved elsewhere and that elsewhere is largely into an area of work where the writer, director and everyone else involved in the production work as collaborators and there is no singular vision but a shared vision.

Over the last 10 years some of the greatest productions by the greatest companies that I've seen have been created in this way. I am thinking of shows such as **Complicite's** *Mnemonic*, **Kneehigh's** *Tristan and Yseult* and *The Red Shoes*, **Improbable's** *70 Hill Lane* and *Coma*, **Theatre-rite's** *Houseworks*, the **National Theatre of Scotland's** *Wolves in the Walls*, **Frantic's** *Dirty Wonderland*, **Forced Entertainment's** *Dirty Work*.

These are productions that in no way ignore the writer and accord the writer their due place at the heart of the creative process - Anna Marie Murphy and Carl Grosse, for example, have undoubtedly done their best work when working collaboratively with director Emma Rice of **Kneehigh** - but they do recognize that the romantic notion of the playwright slaving away alone in the garret to produce a play is just one model available.

It may also be that this collaborative way of working is also more capable of responding to the needs of modern young audiences, who have been brought up in a much more visually sophisticated world than previous generations and who are as likely to respond to the image as they are to the word. I think it is no surprise that **Theatre-rites** and **Oily Cart** who have done some of the most outstanding work in British theatre over the last decade work specifically with audiences - babies and young children - who know nothing of the conventions of theatre and care even less for them; young people with profound and multiple learning disabilities - to whom the word means very little, but who instinctively respond to sound, light, touch, movement and images. Anyone who saw *The Sultan's Elephant* stopping hearts and the traffic in London earlier this year will know that the British public has a previously unsuspected ability to read the encoded deeper meanings in spectacle than anyone might have imagined. Live art is undergoing a regeneration in this country with large numbers of young people flocking to see performances of a form that frequently emerges from the devised and collaborative.

I am not for a moment suggesting that the writer is a dodo on the verge of extinction, and neither am I suggesting that the collaborative process suits all writers and all companies. I have met writers who have been energised by working collaboratively - Mark Ravenhill who has recently worked with **Frantic** on *Pool (No Water)* would be one - but also those who have been crushed.

This is particularly the case with writers who have been unfortunate enough to encounter directors who think that collaboration is an opportunity to reinvent themselves as an auteur. Collaboration must mean exactly what it says - a process in which designer, writer, director, choreographer, actors, lighting and sound designer all have an equal status and opportunity to input into the creative chaos which creates the finished production. It will not work for everyone but, when it does work, it seems to me that it often works in a way that audiences find enormously appealing because the work reaches out and touches them in a way that text based plays often don't.

Theatres have been slow to latch on to this mini-revolution which is taking place. There are many reasons for this. The visual is not nearly as valued in our culture as the word and our new writing theatres are often slow to see beyond the words on the page too.

Emma Rice has recounted that after the success of *Tristan and Yseult* two literary managers at leading theatres admitted that if the text for that production had landed on their desk they would have rejected it out of hand.

She says: "The whole of the establishment is based around the well-made play landing on the desk. Another script of ours was also rejected because the reader said it was 'like a skeleton'. That was the point. It is just a skeleton. The rehearsals put the flesh on."

By its very nature playwrighting is more collaborative than other literary art forms. When I was a young critic in the 1980s one of the reasons often cited for the lack of women playwrights was that while women had no problem writing novels they found the bear pit of the rehearsal room where every word you've written is tested and possibly queried too combative an arena in which to compete.

I'm inclined to think this view was nonsense and it certainly hasn't held back Caryl Churchill, Timberlake Wertenbaker, Debbie Tucker Green, Laura Wade and Tanika Gupta. But I do think that the new world of collaborative writer may encourage a wider access into writing for the theatre than most playwriting schemes will ever muster. At its best, collaborative writing provides a new model for playwrights which pushes the boundaries and allows everyone involved to not just produce their best work but which has a cumulative power greater than the individual parts. And if it does nothing else, it allows playwrights to get out more and engage with the real world beyond their cold lonely garrets and the limits of their own imaginations.

Lyn Gardner

EN MASSE THEATRE - THE SHELTER:
FUN IN STRANGE PLACES

(Clockwise from top) Ingrid Oliver, Dan McGowan & Ross Devlin in The Shelter - Photo by En Masse Theatre

14

John Biddle & Mary Wells in The Shelter - Photo by En Masse Theatre

En Masse is a young company who have made their name by creating award-winning new plays. Their productions are bold, funny and dark, celebrating the creativity of performers and audience alike.

The company was formed by ex-Durham University students **Amy Leach** and **Oliver Birch** in 2003 and has so far produced three productions for children - *The Echo Chamber*, a site-specific ghost story; *The Ignatius Trail*, a pirate musical comedy; and *The Shelter*, a war-time drama.

Here **Oliver Birch**, writer and company member, reveals some of the company's creative touchstones and processes.

The Skeleton Key

THE WORLD OF THE PLAY

When we started creating for young people, one of the first aspects of theatre we wanted to challenge was its conventions. Our first play *The Echo Chamber* began as a ghost tour outside of the venue. The audience were led around the outside of the space, given historical facts and fed bits of information that recurred in the play itself. Finally they were led into the venue and made to stand in the playing space. At an agreed point the lights were extinguished and the 'tour guide' made his exit to apparently fix the faulty fuse. Then the lights slowly faded up to reveal a hooded figure which had appeared among them, who told them to sit down. At this point the Victorian ghost story commenced. The show finished with the 'tour guide' returning and the audience left without applause or having been bowed at.

The Shelter similarly places the audience as partakers of an air raid drill and silent witnesses to a terrible crime. Even *The Ignatius Trail*, a much more conventional piece begins with the eponymous hero adrift, delirious and surrounded by the sound of the ocean. We realised that if we played with the framing conventions of theatre, the audience would be slightly uneasy, but be much more alert and engaged; in other words enchanted by the world of the play. We do not tell children what to think or believe, they are invited into the world and come of their own volition. We found this gives them the independence to watch with keener sight and to form opinions of their own; to claim a stake in what they have seen.

A device which we have employed effectively in the past is that of site-specificity. *The Echo Chamber* was first performed in the former bank vaults of the Bank of Scotland in Edinburgh (now the Underbelly); a claustrophobic and dank room replete with bare stone and bone-gnawing dampness. For *The Shelter*, we transformed the same space into a World War II air raid bunker where the audience sat on ramshackle chairs and patchwork quilts.

The World of the Play has often been our starting point, our frame of reference, helping us to find tone and colour. Once found, we have had the privilege of finding a story which will most interestingly or most completely inhabit this world, of fully exploring our imaginations within those boundaries.

DEVELOPMENT

Our process of development is varied and evolving. We did not begin with a set of fixed ideas about developing new work for children; none of us had an experience of it when we started. It was a process of instinct. We wanted to make a children's play that is entertaining throughout, understandable throughout, which is challenging somehow to young people and, crucially, which we as adult performers would find challenging and fulfilling to perform or, if we were members of the audience, watch.

So our staging, editing, shaping or rehearsing is not involved with what we suppose children might like, or might find frightening or funny, but what we like, are frightened by or find funny. This is central to the work we produce.

(Top) Tiffany Wood; (Middle Row L-R) Ben Smith, Dan McGowan & Dan Lewis; (Bottom Row L-R) John Biddle & Ross Devlin - Photo by En Masse Theatre

Here are some of the tenets which we have stuck to when approaching a new piece :

• The success of our work has been due, in some way, to our innovation and our innovation has been fuelled by the unshakeable belief that children must not be patronised. This is the first tenet upon which we approach our work and so the stories we create are challenging and relentless for young people.

• A good company. We have been working with the same group of actors since the beginning. We have had other actors come and go as with any company but our core group has been present throughout.

• A democratic rehearsal process. When a new script is delivered, it is usually a rough draft and we as a company shape and refine it together. We tend to set aside a considerable amount of time for this; when we are collectively happy with our script we continue. We are not precious about pulling it apart, rewriting or in one case changing the ending. Likewise with direction, we work collectively under the guidance of the director; we have tried to cultivate an atmosphere of inclusion.

• Flexibility when coming to performance. We realised early on that work for young people has to engage its audience possibly more than adult theatre and so the tacit covenant between audience and actors is much stronger. As a result we found it necessary to alter aspects of the performance, sometimes change a word or line, sometimes elucidate slightly. Simply it is a process of tuning in.

• Having fun. It is, I believe, one of the most important aspects of any show to be rooted in enjoyment, from the most dour tragedy to the most absurd farce. We spend a portion of our time playing games and improvising. It is crucial for the cohesion of a company and consequently the cohesion of the story we are telling.

Far more simply, it gives us a large dose of enthusiasm, it helps the energy to remain high and more importantly, allows us to play with each other and return to the children that we were and are. The truth of our productions, as I have said, lies in our ability to express what it is that we as children find exhilarating or challenging or hilarious.

WRITING

When it comes to the writing, I have said that we work from rough drafts. There are also strong themes that I as a writer have been exploring within these plays. The first is the figure of the irresponsible adult. It is a motif I have often returned to. It is a challenge to a child to show an adult who is not exempt from naughtiness or irreverence and also the admonishment which can follow. The second is that of tonal range. By this I mean that I am interested by the polarised nature of human moods and attitudes; that one minute someone can be laughing hysterically and the next they can be terrified and the incredible proximity with which they can exist.

PUSHING OUR CREATIVITY

In short, we want to create work which is a rollercoaster ride, both to watch and perform (one of my most rewarding experiences on the stage was in *The Echo Chamber* regaling a story to an audience of children who might listen intently or stubbornly refuse to be engaged). We believe that an audience should be taken on a wild journey through their emotions, be hurtled through ideas and not be preached at. If our shows are educational, we are careful not to show it; theatre should be alive and relentless, what we learn we learn through enjoyment and wonder. We use no tricks in creating exciting children's theatre, there is only the raw passion for telling the story in the most beautiful or devastating or imaginative way we can think of.

Oliver Birch

19

COMPANY OF ANGELS - VIRGINS:
DIRECTING YOUR OWN WRITING

Tilly Fortune & Stefan Butler in Virgins by Company of Angels
- Photo by Stephen Berkeley-White

Company of Angels has produced some of the most outstanding work for young audiences in the UK over the past five years.

Here **John Retallack** talks about the foundations of the company and also writing and directing *Virgins*, which toured the UK as a co-production with **The Junction (Cambridge)** in Autumn 2006.

COMPANY OF ANGELS

During the period that I was artistic director of **Oxford Stage Company** (1989 – 1999) I won an Arts Council bursary to go and see theatre for children and young people in France, Holland, Italy and Germany. In Holland I went to the *Den Bosch Festival* and saw work of outstanding quality, including *Mirad*, *Boy from Bosnia* and *Hitler's Childhood* (both from **Wederzijds Theatre Company, Amsterdam**), *Bernadettje* from Alain Platel, plus the work of writers and directors like Pauline Mol, Suzanne van Lohuizen, Lisbet Kolthof, Hans van de Boom and, crucially, Ad de Bont.

The week in Den Bosch opened up a new world for me; the work I saw was inspirational. Content was contemporary with a clear political awareness; the acting companies were strong and well-versed in ensemble technique and spirit; viewed simply as theatre it was ravishing – yet shows took place in school gymnasiums in daylight.

The work was strikingly sophisticated and assertively modern in delivery because it had a clear purpose – to intrigue and to entertain young audiences who would soon be citizens with a vote to cast and role to play in the world. These performances surpassed the drab surroundings in which they were placed and gained an almost transcendental theatrical power in doing so.

I wrote at the time of one performance, **Wederzijds'** production of *Hitler's Childhood*:

> *This was really inspirational theatre on an issue that refuses to be buried. Adults know everything about the end of Hitler, but who knows about the beginning? Is a fascist born evil or is he made evil by his upbringing and surroundings? These seem important questions in a part of Belgium where the Vlaams Blok is winning so many votes. This performance was accurately judged and conceived with great imagination and intelligence. It was also very beautiful to look at and to listen to. It was the most original work I've seen all year. It makes theatre for young people a fresh prospect and makes me speculate if it might be an exciting step to take personally.*

Oxford Stage Company and **Wederzijds** worked together frequently between 1993 and 1998 and the relationship with Ad de Bont continues still.

In 1995, with **Oxford Stage Company**, I introduced the first of two programmes of new work for young people in England called *Making the Future*.

The project presented European texts in translation; in 1998 a second *Making the Future* programme of newly commissioned English work (including my adaptation of *Junk* by Melvyn Burgess) was toured throughout the UK.

Susan Benn, the director of **Performing Arts Labs (PAL)** then invited me to run a ten-day *Lab* for a dozen young writers of new plays for young people. The first one in 1996 led to five further *Labs* and the writing - over a five year period - of forty new plays for young audiences, many of which have been subsequently produced.

In 2000, I was vexed that I couldn't persuade any writer to write the type of play I wanted to direct for young people. I think I wanted to write what I called a 'Dutch' play but in an English idiom. This was *Hannah and Hanna* – my first play, co-produced with **Channel Theatre Company** in May 2001 and played at the Edinburgh Fringe Festival.

Hannah and Hanna allowed me to form what I had been planning since I left **Oxford Stage Company** in 1999 – a company that would promote new and experimental work for young audiences. I named it **Company of Angels** not only because it would have to multiply on a wing and a prayer - but because I thought that Angels could turn up anywhere at anytime.

At this time I wrote a brief statement of the company's approach:

> • *Much of the political and emotional centre of social change in our society revolves around children and young people.*

> • *Theatre has a counter-cultural identity when it is prepared to leave its familiar audiences and buildings behind.*

> • *Theatre to young 'non-theatre' audiences in 'non-theatre' spaces can stimulate avant-garde work of originality and beauty.*

> • *Writers, directors, dancers, designers, artists and actors can all reveal startling new horizons when they adopt or challenge the world view of, say, an eight-year old or a fifteen-year old.*

> • *Theatre 'for young people' is often depicted wrongly as if it were itself a 'junior' art form.*

Teresa Ariosto joined as Producer in January 2002 and we became an Arts Council revenue client in April 2004.

Teresa and I wrote the following mission for the company:

> • *To foster and produce new and experimental theatre work for young audiences addressing key aspects of social change.*

VIRGINS

Virgins is a play about taboo. I think that this is why there is dance in it – there are things that people are feeling strongly but that they cannot say to each other. This affects their body language and how they behave towards one another.

I read an academic paper that says English and American families tend to dramatize adolescent sexuality (highlight negative risks and speak ominously about the consequences - pregnancy, infection, effect of drugs, etc) and, for example, Dutch and Scandinavian families who normalize it; that is, they talk openly about their sexual lives, accommodate the changes and see no cause for over-reaction. It's clear to me the same adolescent will behave quite differently if he or she is subject to one or the other of these two approaches.

The drama of the play comes out of a culture that dramatizes sexuality rather than normalizing it – Jack's wild night at the party is a response. A 'Dutch' family would have talked through the pointlessness of a night like that long ago. Jack's family are reactive but unable to open up the subject until it has become a source of conflict. I think the family will adapt as a result but hurts and slights live on a very long time in a family's memory.

Although I wrote a lot more text for this play – especially the parents and their feelings towards each other – in the end I decided to go with making the family as unspecific as possible in naturalistic terms. I wanted the audience to place themselves into the family and into this situation – from what people have said I think that this has worked.

One other key aspect is the sexuality of the parents themselves. Adolescents have a natural urge to place their own dramas centre stage – but if the family is a happy one there will be a sexual narrative going on with the parents as well.

At certain points in a family's life there is quite a lot of sexual energy under one roof. English houses are quite small and all the bedrooms are usually on the same floor. I feel those northern Europeans must be truly cool-blooded to normalize everything as effectively as they do.

It is easy to imagine that a writer/director is a very clear individual who knows exactly what he or she wants. That might be true in the end but in my case I very much need the help of every one involved to get to that point. Fleur Darkin had a big input as did Liz Cooke the designer. Understanding emotion in terms of dance is truly difficult. Fleur rejected many ideas before settling on what exists in the final show. We were fortunate to have actors who danced so confidently – though there is not more than 10 minutes of dance in the show, choreography took up 70% of rehearsal time. The actors also contributed a great deal, especially Stefan Butler who played Jack in both the **Soho** and the **Lyric Theatre** readings.

The play was written over an 18 month period and I was always nervous that people would just say, 'So what?' I'm sure some people do but it seems to speak to adults as well as teenagers and it is now about to be translated into French and German. But not Swedish or Dutch I think...

Stefan Butler in Virgins by Company of Angels
Photo by Stephen Berkeley-White

WHAT HAVE I LEARNT THROUGH DOING THIS PLAY?

• I have learnt that there are more ways of doing it than the one we chose – perhaps I will do a new version of it in 2008 with different music, different dances, more speeches by the parents.

• I also learnt – once again - that the greater the personal investment in a play, the greater the nerves that you experience every day.

• It is good to listen to everyone and to take soundings all the time from people who watch runs of the play and so on – but ultimately, as writer/director, only you know what you really want (much as you wish someone would tell you what it is you want)

• That the choice of music is all important. We rejected so many good tunes and songs before settling on that fractious bit of John Adams.

• I also learnt that what may be a great dance in isolation may not work in the context of the play – and what may seem dry in isolation, may be great in context.

• The last thing I have to write (or it would amount to an untruth not to write it), is that I've learnt so much from my wife, not just in bringing up our children but in this business of talking about plays. She is a fine dramaturg, no less or more on this play than on every other one I've written. So, to Nina, many thanks.

John Retallack

TRAVELLING LIGHT - MOTHER SAVAGE:
WRITING WITHOUT WORDS

Dan Canham in Mother Savage - Photo by Graham Burke

Travelling Light is one of the UK's leading theatre companies making theatre for young audiences. The company produces new work, either devised, adapted or from commissioned scripts, with a performance style which is physical, visual and musical.

In 2006 the company successfully combined a devising and writing process, collaborating with writer **Hattie Naylor**. Here **Mike Akers**, Education Director, describes what happened.

WRITING WITHOUT WORDS

Travelling Light's 2006 production of *Mother Savage* was based on a short story of the same name by Guy de Maupassant. The original tale was written in 1884 and is set during the Franco Prussian war. It tells the story of a widowed peasant woman whose son is away fighting at the front. Four enemy soldiers are billeted with her when the Prussian Army occupies her village. Over time they strike up a mutually beneficial, almost cordial relationship, until a letter arrives to tell her that her boy has been killed in action at the front, and fills her head with thoughts of retribution.

The company had worked with writers in numerous different ways in the past, but this process was to be an entirely new one. Initially Hattie Naylor was not employed as the writer. She was brought into the creative team with a brief to shape and structure material being created during a devising process and was given the title of dramaturg.

From the outset director, Craig Edwards was keen to explore the possibilities of telling this moving story using only two actors and with a minimum of words. The protagonists speak different languages and one of the key themes is about their common humanity superseding differences of language and culture. Did we really need a writer when planning to use so few words?

Craig explains: "Writing doesn't have to be about words. Hattie believes this too. The actors' physical relationship with the space, each other and the audience can speak volumes. It's about allowing the words, the music and the movement to happen so they complement each other, so they work in harmony."

With a background in painting and visual art and a strong track record of working with dance companies, Hattie entirely agreed that this story needed to be told as economically as possible. "Text had to be dragged out of me," she says. It was an unusual experience for Hattie to enter a rehearsal period not only without a script, but also without any preconceived ideas about how this story might be realised on stage.

Almost all Hattie's writing was done in the rehearsal room. This was a script that grew out of a collaborative ethic, rather than one that was created in isolation by the writer alone with her word processor and her vision of how this story might be brought to life. However, by the end of the process, Hattie's title had changed from dramaturg to writer, mainly because she had written all of the dialogue spoken in the play. "The improvisations were a great source of material, but they were too loose for this piece. To make room for all the music, movement and silence, the dialogue needed to be pared back and made completely tight, which was where my writing skills were needed," she says.

Maggie Tagney in Mother Savage - Photo by Graham Burke

Initially there was some concern about the ownership of the script. Was it fair that the writer should take all the credit for a script that the whole team had created, and which finally consisted largely of stage directions? A decision was made that copyright would be shared equally among all contributors.

As the process evolved, the importance of having a voice in the room with a brief to shape the play's structure and give significance to every one of the limited number of words used became clear. It was Hattie who pushed for the play to be underpinned by a strong three act structure. She was able to say "You can't have another scene here," or "'this section lacks narrative drive," if she felt it necessary.

The production had a large creative team including the director, writer, designer, lighting designer, choreographer, music director, producer and two actors. With so many voices in the rehearsal room the success of the project depended heavily on the director's ability to handle a large team. "Craig managed the team brilliantly," says Hattie, "he created such a positive bond between us that we were all able to be open". Part of the strategy to achieve this involved warm ups and team exercises that everyone in the room took part in. A structure for how different members of the team fed into the creative process gradually evolved. Hattie became a kind of second in command, able to be vocal and given authority by Craig's confidence in her, and working in harmony with him to realise what was by now a shared vision.

Mother Savage toured to schools and mid scale venues in spring 2006. The show was a huge success and received rapturous responses both from schools and public audiences. The process of making the play was enormously positive for **Travelling Light**.

Artistic Producer Jude Merrill says: "Hattie made an invaluable contribution to this production. Her ability to see the play as a whole and to shape and structure the narrative were crucial in making the piece such an emotionally engaging one".

This was a brave play to present to young teenagers since it demands their concentration through long periods without dialogue, but the warmth of their response proved that it worked. The process will have a lasting impact on our future work.

Mike Akers

ACTION TRANSPORT - THE BOMB:
A FICTION BASED ON FACT

Action Transport: A fiction based on fact

Jo Berry & Pat Magee (foreground) with The Bomb cast Autumn 2006 -
Paul Dodds, Janet Bamford, Richard Walker, Sally Evans - Photo by Sylvia Selzer

Action Transport has a growing interest in creating plays connected to real events. In 2006 the company produced *The Bomb*, a new play inspired by **Jo Berry**, whose father was killed in the 1984 Brighton Bomb, and **Pat Magee**, the man who planted it.

Here we look at three aspects of the production: the real events which inspired the play, **Kevin Dyer's** approach as writer and the role of the commissioner.

THE FACTS

When Sir Anthony Berry MP was killed in the IRA Brighton Bombing during the 1984 Tory Party Conference, his daughter Jo was thrown into a conflict she knew very little about. Since then she has visited Ireland many times and worked with victims and former combatants from all sides. In November 2000 she met Pat Magee, the man responsible for her father's death.

Belfast-born Pat Magee, former IRA activist, was given multiple life sentences for the Brighton Bombing. Released under the Good Friday Agreement in 1999, he has since been actively involved in peace work.

JO BERRY

An inner shift is required to hear the story of the enemy. For me the question is always about whether I can let go of my need to blame, and open my heart enough to hear Pat's story and understand his motivations. The truth is that sometimes I can and sometimes I can't. It's a journey and it's a choice, which means it's not all sorted and put away in a box.

It felt as if a part of me died in that bomb. I was totally out of my depth but somehow I held on to a small hope that something positive would come out of the trauma. So I went to Ireland and listened to the stories of many remarkable and courageous people who'd been caught up in the violence. For the first time I felt that my pain was being heard.

In those early years I probably used the word 'forgiveness' too liberally – I didn't really understand it. When I used the word on television, I was shocked to receive a death threat from a man who said I had betrayed both my father and my country.

Now I don't talk about forgiveness. To say "I forgive you" is almost condescending – it locks you into an 'us and them' scenario keeping me right and you wrong. That attitude won't change anything. But I can experience empathy, and in that moment there is no judgement. Sometimes when I've met with Pat, I've had such a clear understanding of his life that there's nothing to forgive.

I wanted to meet Pat to put a face to the enemy, and see him as a real human being. At our first meeting I was terrified, but I wanted to acknowledge the courage it had taken him to meet me. We talked with an extraordinary intensity. I shared a lot about my father, while Pat told me some of his story.

Over the past two and a half years of getting to know Pat, I feel I've been recovering some of the humanity I lost when that bomb went off. Pat is also on a journey to recover his humanity. I know that he sometimes finds it hard to live with the knowledge that he cares for the daughter of someone he killed through his terrorist actions.

Perhaps more than anything I've realised that no matter which side of the conflict you're on, had we all lived each others lives, we could all have done what the other did. In other words, had I come from a Republican background, I could easily have made the same choices Pat made.

32

PAT MAGEE

Some day I may be able to forgive myself. Although I still stand by my actions, I will always carry the burden that I harmed other human beings. But I'm not seeking forgiveness. If Jo could just understand why someone like me could get involved in the armed struggle then something has been achieved. The point is that Jo set out with that intent in mind – she wanted to know why.

I decided to meet Jo because, apart from addressing a personal obligation, I felt obligated as a Republican to explain what led someone like me to participate in the action. I told her that I'd got involved in the armed struggle at the age of 19, after witnessing how a small nationalist community were being mistreated by the British. Those people had to respond. For 28 years I was active in the Republican Movement. Even in jail I was still a volunteer.

Between Jo and I, the big issue is the use of violence. I can't claim to have renounced violence, though I don't believe I'm a violent person and have spoken out against it. I am 100% in favour of the peace process, but I am not a pacifist and I could never say to future generations, anywhere in the world, who felt themselves oppressed, "Take it, just lie down and take it."

Jo told me that her daughter had said after one of our meetings, "Does that mean that Grandad Tony can come back now?" It stuck with me, because of course nothing has fundamentally changed. No matter what we can achieve as two human beings meeting after a terrible event, the loss remains and forgiveness can't embrace that loss. The hope lies in the fact that we are prepared to carry on. The dialogue has continued.

It's rare to meet someone as gracious and open as Jo. She's come a long way in her journey to understanding; in fact, she's come more than half way to meet me. That's a very humbling experience.

Article included with the kind permission of The Forgiveness Project –
© **www.theforgivenessproject.com**

Kevin Dyer - Photo by Sylvia Selzer

THE STORY

I'm used to writing 'imagination' plays. That is, some idea pops into my head, then supporting material is dredged up from somewhere inside me, and then it's all grappled into shape by some intellectual understanding (possibly) of structure and character and how to tell a story in a theatre.

The Bomb is a bit different to the previous plays I've written. I was driving along listening to 'Woman's Hour' and I heard Jo Berry being interviewed.

Jo's dad was killed in the Brighton bombing. An IRA bomb-maker planted a bomb in The Grand Hotel, Brighton. He was using new technology, a timer that he could set three weeks before the bomb goes off. So he checked into the hotel, planted the bomb and left – his aim was to destroy the British government.

I didn't really know all that when I listened to Jo Berry.

What I did know was: that morning, when I heard her talk about wanting to meet the man who planted the bomb that killed her dad, I was listening to something profound, personal, political. She was talking about something intensely moving that connected to my own life.

This need to meet her dad's killer picked away at Jo Berry for many years. She worked at this need, on and off until, nearly twenty years later, she made it happen.

Since then she and Pat Magee have met and become friends.

Janet Bamford and Paul Dodds in The Bomb - Photo by Sylvia Selzer

So, how would I write a play about all that?

On that day I was driving to Ellesmere Port for a day at the **Action Transport** office. I arrived and sort of blurted out, probably not very coherently, some stuff about the interview I had just heard. Joe Sumsion was pretty prompt. "You should write that," he said. And commissioned me there and then.

I didn't know what the play was going to be like. I had no picture of it in my head. But I knew that I had to meet Jo Berry.

I did that. Several times. In London at the place where she sought refuge after the bomb went off; at her home; on a beach. I wanted to know everything she would tell me about the bomb, the night it went off, afterwards, before, her family, meeting Pat Magee, everything.

I also knew I had to convince her that I would not betray her, that I would not 'use' her story like some arty tabloid. I had to promise her that I would let her see the material I wrote – without promising her that she could re-write any of it.

Once I'd spoken and listened to her, I had to meet Pat Magee. It was clear that the stuff of the play was his story as well as her story. I had to make the same promises to him, not out of expediency but because I thought it was the right thing to do.

So I read all the stuff in the public domain, I spoke to people to gauge their reaction to the emerging story. I kept asking myself, 'What is the story? What is the story?'

And then came the writing of it, the sifting and the selection. Because that's what writing a story is, isn't it – a choosing of what to tell.

But in this instance there was a twist. I knew that using real events and real words could have a powerful veracity. But I also know that unedited life is pretty boring, and the way to make Jo and Pat's 'story' into an unforgettable night in the theatre was the melding of real lives and theatrical jiggery-pokery.

I knew that many in my audience (it is a play for 14 years plus) wouldn't know where Brighton was, never mind all that political stuff of 20 years ago. For them the only 'truth' was the one they were going to see from 7.30 pm and for the next 64 minutes.

So, to free myself from the obligation to Pat and Jo I had to work out why I was writing the play – and it became clear it wasn't principally for them. There came a point when I had to stop asking Pat and Jo for permission and for corroboration.

I stopped writing to them, ringing them, thinking of them almost, and wrote what the play needed, not what the people needed.

Then I could start using all that imaginative stuff, and to start borrowing from my father's life and my partner's life and one of the young women in the **Action Transport Young Writers' Group** – who became the model for the character of Marnie - and my own childhood.

It's like when you write a scene in a play. You work out the function/beats/structure of the scene, but then park that analysis and get on and write it. As I created characters based on the lives of Jo Berry and Pat Magee - but not them - I could make them less iconic, more flawed. Just changing the names allowed me to keep certain essences, use 'facts' and real dialogue, but mix it up a bit with what the story needed.

So, what do we end up with? A fiction based on fact; a story based on truth that has its own truth. And the truth of fiction can be stronger than the truth of a real life event - because the artist is focussing so much time, resources, effort into choosing and clarifying her/his statement. Life is more random.

When we got to first draft, the two of them came sharply back into focus. And I remember my hands shaking as I met Jo soon after she had read the script. Pat did have a problem with one scene, and I did take it out – he thought it was factually incorrect, and politically misleading. Interestingly, all the bits that have gone in the play that are recollections and re-makings of my own life as a young man have proved no problem to him.

One day in rehearsals: it was an unforgettable time sitting next to Jo Berry whose dad was killed in the bomb and Pat Magee who planted it as we all watched the scene where the bomb goes off. Never have I been so aware that one of the greatest relationships in the theatre is that between individual audience member and individual audience member as they experience a play that is about them.

Kevin Dyer

COMMISSIONING 'THE BOMB'

I doubt that there are any rules for being a successful commissioner or dramaturg – like most things I think you learn by your mistakes.

I used to think that the role was about 'solving' plays – assessing the weaknesses and working out how to fix them. Increasingly I now think it is about finding talented writers with original ideas, working out how they tick, then creating the circumstances in which they can flourish. I like the phrase 'creative personal bests' – I certainly think that both Kevin and I achieved these on *The Bomb*, which I'm sure is a major contributing factor to its success.

My touchstones for working on *The Bomb* were:

Pre-first draft

• Being clear with the writer on the company's expectations of the commission.

• Committing enough of my time to the process.

• Shielding the writer from unhelpful influences – commissioners and not writers should deal with funding pressures, unhelpful opinions, interference.

• Listening to the writer. Kevin often knew what he needed to help him get to the next stage; I tried to provide it.

Joe Sumsion and Julian Ronnie (Composer) in The Bomb rehearsals - Photo by Sylvia Selzer

• Committing to the writer's vision. I tried to help Kevin write his play, not the play I might have written or the one I might have wished he'd written.

• Looking after the writer. Reminding Kevin and others that creating great works of art is often a fragile process.

• Remembering the audience. Most writers will at some point lose sight of the audience; the commissioner can gently bring the audience back into focus.

Post-first draft

• Running two development days with actors and a designer. This allowed us to test out the first draft, seeing what worked (about 60%), what didn't, where the gaps and possibilities were.

• Bringing lots of opinions, ideas and responses into the process. Plays shouldn't be written by committee but often benefit from many inputs. Many people read drafts and fed back to me; I was a filter for this, clearly structuring feedback as the single voice of the company.

• Giving detailed, specific feedback in writing. This covered strengths, areas for attention and possibilities for development, including 'what if?' scenarios. I tried to give feedback which could be easily understood and acted upon; I tried to avoid vague criticism, which writers hate.

• Prioritising doggedness, attention to detail and my own stamina. Often plays will need to go to five or six drafts, as this one did.

Joe Sumsion

HALF MOON - LOCKED IN:
SEARCHING FOR THE AUTHENTIC VOICE

Ashley J in Locked In - Photo by Sylvia Selzer

40

Ashley J as Blaze and Kim Lee Hardy as Tariq - Photo by Patrick Baldwin
Extract from Locked In © Fin Kennedy 2006

LOCKED IN - EXTRACT

BLAZE	Yo yo yo! Big up da East London massive!
	It's dat time again!
	Yeah! Yeah! Yeah! Bring it on!
	Yo it's MC Blaze on da mike controllin
	Always hit a strike like I'm ten-pin bowlin
	If yu playin Keeper den I'll always get a goal in
	Rhymes rock steady like a boulder in da dark
	I can smell yu fear like a Great White Shark
	Or should dat be Great Black cos white ain't always right
	But whateva - you're da meat an I'm gonna take a bite
	(He makes a biting manouvre towards ZAHIDA)
ZAHIDA	Get off man!
TARIQ	Ssh.
ZAHIDA	He's tryin a chirps me!
BLAZE	Yo yo yo! Big up people!
TARIQ	Big yous all up!
BLAZE	Da East End massive!
TARIQ	Da Stepney gals an boys!
BLAZE	Swanlea, Mulberry, make some noise!
TARIQ	Messin up da airwaves, loud an proud
BLAZE	Crankin up da tunes for da East End crowd
TARIQ	It's Exile FM
BLAZE	Ninety-two point ten and you're locked into
B & T	Da Two Wise Men!
BLAZE	Yo yo yo! Big shout out to all da regular
	massives locked in
TARIQ	Yu know who yu are
BLAZE	And for those a yu dat don't know
TARIQ	Dis is how it goes
BLAZE	We're London's leadin
TARIQ	Talk at speedin
BLAZE	Fastest breedin
TARIQ	Leave yu bleedin
BLAZE	Hip-hoppin
TARIQ	Non-stoppin
BLAZE	Body poppin
TARIQ	Rhyme droppin
BLAZE	Nanginest
TARIQ	Banginest
BLAZE	Blinginest
TARIQ	Minginest
BLAZE	Telephone ringinest
B & T	Phone-in show!

Based in the East End of London, **Half Moon** has developed working processes designed to reflect the voices and concerns of their local community. In 2006 the company produced *Locked In*, an ambitious play set in the world of pirate radio.

Here **Chris Elwell**, the company's Director, reveals the process of commissioning, developing and producing the work.

PROCESS

Over the past three years our writers have emerged from our 'pool' of freelance artists. These artists have been attracted to **Half Moon** because of our work and have been employed as workshop leaders across our participatory portfolio – working in our schools, our youth theatres and so on. They all have three things in common. They are wanting to:

• explore and place language at the heart of their creativity;

• engage with the emotional maturity of our young audiences;

• understand and work in direct contact and consultation with young people during a writing development period.

Usually, as tutors, they will have already written short plays for the young people to perform themselves – *Performanceworks* and *Scriptworks* being our most popular programmes. Here, we place the writer alongside an experienced theatre tutor and designer for up to sixteen hours of direct contact with young people.

At the end of this process, a 'play' is presented by the young people to their peers and the script published – albeit in a simple photocopied booklet format. At this point, a writer may well have something they want to say. Importantly, the writer has been inspired by the young people to tell 'their' story. It is at this point that a writer will be offered a commission.

Commissioning at this time may simply be:

• a 'translation' of the twelve or twenty hander 'play' into a more focussed small-scale piece often to be realised by two to four actors;

• simple treatments of ideas based on the encounter or similar experiences and observations;

• a selection of script extracts equally inspired.

These are offered up to our young people once again through our range of participatory programmes to explore, pull apart or to be used as a stimulus for their own creative work. Their reaction and response is observed by the writer. The creative continuum has begun - a fusion between the participatory work and the writer's creative processes.

In due course, a full script will emerge. This will be read to focus groups in our local schools, or presented as rehearsed readings for our youth theatres to critique. Although at the end – usually having produced four drafts in total - **Half Moon** would want the option to produce the play as one of our two annual national tours, it is the process and the nurturing of writers that underpins the work with writers. Producing the commission is not the overbearing goal. Such pressures can stifle innovation and reduce risk-taking.

Kim Lee Hardy as Tariq - Photo by Patrick Baldwin

LOCKED IN

It is within this context that *Locked In* emerged. Over a three and half year period, with myself as the dramaturg, initially as a series of monologues developed through a *Scriptworks* programme with Year 10 students from Mulberry Girls School, E1 (*East End Tales*); to *B-Minor*, a short play looking at a suicide bombing in Leicester Square through the eyes of three bystanders, used as a stimulus for *Careers-in-Theatre* (a borough-wide Y10 'play in a day' programme); repeated with extracts from draft 1 of *Locked In* for the same programme a year later; then a full reading of draft 2 to Half Moon's senior youth theatre quickly followed by a full rehearsed reading for Year 11 students at Swanlea Community School, E1 of draft 3; the unexpected influence of the London bombings on July 7th 2005; a full script development day with actors and the designated director for the production, Angela Micheals, and then the inevitable edits and re-works as the play is rehearsed.

So what of the play itself? *Locked In* toured nationally from September through November 2006. The world is set on the 20th floor of an abandoned East End tower block, where a Caribbean MC and Bengali DJ rip up the airwaves on a leading pirate station. These two 16 year olds are sick of people telling them what to do – go to school, do your exams - and that people don't recognise their talent or understand them. Then Zahida (of mixed Pakistani-Trinidadian heritage) comes into their lives.

Although directly connecting thematically with Islamic fundamentalism and gun crime, the thrust of the play is a human experience exploring the struggle for identity or finding one's true voice, making choices and friendship – a 'coming of age' in a world where (given the characters' troubled backgrounds), falling into the stereotype can seem to be the only option.

The piece uses a certain lifestyle, that of hip hop and pirate radio, a very specific and contemporary medium, as the frame of the action.

There are three potent symbols in the play: a camera, a gun and a knife. These are invested with equal weight, ensuring that they were all equally seductive, so that the audience comes to see that ultimately the potency comes not from these instruments but the choices we make about how we use them.

Zahida, the character who contains the voice of reason and has the broadest perspective on life, is the casualty of this 'hot-house' atmosphere and implosion. Dealing with this dramatic loss without sentimentality is the play's biggest challenge. The play aims to realise a legacy of hope, showing that the two boys have broken from the constraints of their limited thinking and have made positive choices in their lives. Importantly, *Locked In* invokes stereotypes, but it does so in order to take on those who are so irresponsibly peddling them. It does so in order to say to audiences of all ages that there is another way.

FEEDBACK

"I thought theatre was boring but I have changed my mind – this is real, the lyrics were so real, I know these people - when can I see it again?"
Student, 16, E14

"...a rare moment in my teaching career – the young people understood every word, every moment, and were deeply moved at the girl's death – I looked on and realised that while I didn't understand everything, they totally did."
Teacher, Oaklands School, E1

*"**Locked In** is an example of that rare, beautiful creature: a youth-marketed play that really does make a connection with its audience. Totally gripping and realistic."*
Croydon Advertiser 13/10/06

"Kennedy has a highly attuned ear for the patter of local kids and understanding of tribal loyalties. Angela Michaels' production is steely, and the young cast live and breathe their roles... the show has you in its grip."
The Guardian 20/10/06

ABOUT HALF MOON

For a professional theatre company like **Half Moon**, which engages specifically with young people from birth to 17, our responsibility is to engage meaningfully and respond honestly to our audiences and participants, and to grow and change accordingly. *Locked In* by Fin Kennedy, like many of our commissions, began at a moment where the authentic voice of our community and our audiences spoke directly to an artist who had the skills to frame and broker their stories and aspirations into a piece of theatre.

Half Moon Young People's Theatre aims to produce and present professional theatre for and with young people that informs, challenges and shapes their artistic potential, placing these creative experiences at the core of our policies and practices. The company presents all its work under one artistic umbrella, ensuring a cohesion of all its activities and so providing an interlocking dialogue and exchange between the two areas of activity:

• Professional Theatre - producing and presenting professional theatre at the base, in venues and in youth and schools settings

• Participatory Programme - providing an extensive participatory programme including youth theatres, school and community projects

The company principally serves London and works exclusively with young people from birth to age 17, placing a particular emphasis upon engaging those often excluded in terms of culture (ethnicity) and ability (disability). Annually over 32,000 individuals participate in the full range of activities, 59.9% of users are from Black and Minority Ethnic groups, 59% are female and 9% are disabled. **Half Moon** is a regular funded client of Arts Council London, London Councils and Tower Hamlets, with further financial support from many trusts and foundations and commercial sources.

Chris Elwell

Charles Way has written over forty plays, many of them for children and young people, and his work has been produced all over the world. He has won numerous awards, including The Children's Award from **Arts Council England** for his play *Red Red Shoes*.

At *The Lockpickers' Ball* festival in 2006 he talked frankly about his journey as a writer and his efforts to improve the quality of his own writing. This is what he said.

There are many ways in which theatre for children and young people can be improved and over the past few years this subject has had a lot of attention and as a result many proposals have been discussed and some initiated. These include training initiatives, co-productions, overseas trips to see other ways of working and of course the never ending and proper demand for increased funding in this sector. But today I'm not going to talk about money directly. We know that investment will lead to more opportunities and proportionally better work, but the equation between more money and higher quality theatre is no simple one. Today I'd like to consider 'quality' from a personal angle in regard to improving the quality of my own work, which may reflect outward to some larger issues.

I have often described myself as a person who writes plays for children but I have begun to wonder if I write plays for children at all - maybe it's a disguise and I just pretend to? Truer to say perhaps that I write plays for myself, with children in mind, hoping that they'll like the same stories and ways of telling stories that I do. Essentially I am always writing about what bugs me, what concerns me and I've come to realise that I have no other honest option. The child in the audience I'm addressing is really the child in me.

RAISING QUALITY IN YOUNG PEOPLE'S THEATRE

Charles Way - Photo by Sylvia Selzer

So this is a stumbling journey through the idea of 'improving the quality' of my own offerings as a writer involved in the daily business of quality control; deciding what's good or bad, what's better than, what to write about and what forms to use.

The successful play is one in which the playwright has made the best choices the optimum amount of times, which may sound simplistic but is basically true. It was very hard as a young playwright in 1977 to choose the best option the optimum amount of times because I didn't have a history of mistakes and successes to build on. It's in the doing, the failing and succeeding, where the journey of quality control begins. In my early plays I had a distinct inclination to allow characters to overstay their welcome just because they had something which 'I' not 'they' wanted to say. I would in the classic way tell rather than show.

Why is this such a hard lesson to learn? I now think that my early stuff wasn't actually theatre. I was engaged in writing a kind of pretend theatre - based upon what I 'thought' theatre was for rather than what it physically is. Therefore much time was spent sidestepping theatre's real potential and my own. It took at least ten years, to find my personal dramatic voice, my literary self, one which others would recognise and say yes, I know who wrote that, and it is theatre.

COLLECTIVE WORKING

I've been a professional playwright now for nearly thirty years which takes us back to flares, sideburns and the 'collective devising process'. Along the route from that specific creative process to now I have steadily given more and more attention to getting something right or true from the personal sense, examining more closely the complexities of human behaviour. In the early 'collective' work I was just one of the creative voices making a play and the complexities of human behaviour took second place to the issues of the time. And although I was totally committed personally and intellectually to our creative process even then I felt somewhat out of place, engaged in a strange two-dimensional world; us against fascism, us against cuts to nurses pay, us against multinational companies. What defined our collective voice was being in opposition. In itself this was no bad thing; I was young and wanted to change things and wanted to use theatre to do so, as a consequence what I perceived as 'quality' theatre then was somewhat different to now.

When I began writing for professional Theatre-In-Education the objectives of our plays or 'programmes' were very tangible. We, as a group, would try to create something which gripped the audience not through detailed character study in a Dickensian sense, but in a Brechtian mode whereby characters would be defined by outer forces working upon them.

These forces corresponded to our own social political belief system which we'd spent many meetings defining. If it sounds that I am belittling this process I am not. Some of this work was very strong and laid open to me the basic workings of theatre in an 'empty space'. I could see what gripped the audience and what didn't. When the plays became laboured and preachy they became impotent.

The collective devising process provided me with a working critical viewpoint; somewhere from which I could start judging what was 'better than' in regards to the various aspects of theatre.

I started to write plays, however, long before I had any political or social motives that I was aware of, when I was 14 years old. I felt compelled to write and I don't know why. Everything I saw in the theatre was neither good or bad it simply was and it is wonderful as a young person to be free of the weight of too much knowledge because it meant I was able to receive and respond instinctively. It's impossible and unhealthy to stay in such blissful ignorance because one must develop a critical sense.

Sometimes, however, I have seen the open mindedness of the young misused by letting ourselves get away with work that either isn't finished or hasn't been considered deeply enough. Our work can go 'wrong' and once one develops 'standards' and notions of 'quality' it's no longer a purely relative thing. I hate to hear good criticism of children's theatre answered with "Oh but the children loved it". Of course they do, they're not expecting or hoping for something better. Teachers sometimes think they are defending theatre workers in a supporting way when they say this but a lot of teachers themselves can't tell the difference between good theatre and poor theatre. They tend to watch the children not the theatre, and so suspend their own critical faculties. Teacher and child deserve work that is emotionally, visually and intellectually strong and I need to keep demanding this of my own work.

CRITICISM

One way to judge or place one's own offerings is to go and see lots of other people's work and from time to time I go foraging. **Out of Joint** describe themselves as a company who interacts and makes work with other 'top end' companies, meaning **The Royal Court** and the **National Theatre**. So who are the 'top end' companies of the moment in YPT - the companies whom people know produce quality work? And what is the nature of their work and what makes it so?

It's very difficult and sometimes upsetting to decide that one's own work just isn't good enough and it's harder to make clear judgements without an objective, if there ever can be, standard to follow. Due to the lack of critical debate surrounding YPT one has to create one's own standard, and that's hard. Our profession needs another ten critics like Lyn Gardner to debate the merits and faults of the eclectic band of companies that represent British YPT. We need ten because then you have debate rather than opinion. Without debate we fall back on our instincts and that makes it hard to see the new in a positive light.

In setting my own standards I have of course loved every good review but I've probably learned more from the bad ones. Twenty years ago I took reviews personally - not so much now because I'm more confident - although you can't function as an artist without self doubt - and bad reviews will stimulate that but more importantly they stimulate self examination, and force one to see one's own work from a distance. I have tried to make this journey away from myself in an effort to clear the mind of stumbling blocks, of which vanity is surely the greatest. This struggle with one's own personality is one I engage in every time I write. We writers tend to like the sound of our own voices, a trait more forgivable in novelists than playwrights.

I look increasingly to find that writing place where I am a vehicle for my own small talent not an encumbrance. It is very easy to obstruct one's own talent. My worst fault is the desire to be liked, a fault which disables characters as they try to be reflections of myself and mouth pieces for generalised notions that I hold dear - but the characters may not.

One can learn to criticise and praise one's self to a certain degree but others have a crucial role to play, not least the audience, in whom I place some, though not all, my trust and who often differ from the 'critic'. Praise is part of criticism and is more important than we'd like to acknowledge - believing it to be somehow childish - but we need it because writing is hard work - and if it isn't hard you're either a genius or just not very good.

POLITICS

The late seventies was a time of political conflict and class struggle and in the theatre companies I worked for we spent many hours in political debate, but the greatest personal influence on my writing was the debate about gender and gender politics. Writers need these debates - particularly playwrights because of the very social nature of the end event. These days I have to force myself to have the debates internally and abstractly. I use the play itself to find out about my own attitudes. As a writer/director today I will often try to rediscover that level of engagement with those I work with by placing the text to one side - and asking the team to engage not only with the script but the world we live in, the world in which the production will finally exist. Do they think they can bring about change? Where would this change occur, internally - or externally? Are they optimistic or pessimistic about the power of theatre - and how can these questions influence or act upon how we produce the play? The question finally is, why do this play - now?

As a process, the collective creative way sometimes led to work which contained too many voices and ideas and therefore the work produced varied in quality. David Holman, a fine writer, found a way of writing his own plays within the collective structure and honed a style by shedding unneeded material that made the themes within the plays sharp and visible. Gradually it became clear that quality was improved when the devising group let the individual flourish and find their individual skills - whether in design, writing or directing.

For myself I need time to dream, which may sound a touch pretentious but for me playwrighting isn't the wholly conscious thing I may have made it sound. I need time and space to make connections in the way that a poet makes connections between words, images and ideas that surprise the reader.

COLLABORATION

In the area of new writing, Paul Swift, Mike Kenny and Greg Cullen among many others all learned their craft through the devising process and found their own unique theatrical voices. The practical day-to-day experience of making and putting on plays, one after the other, was invaluable. It seems we now have to find and provide a new format to allow others to enter this creative playmaking world.

In the absence of actor-led groups providing a practical theatre making structure for writers to grow within, the role of the director/producer has become more important; the person who creates situations for other artists in which to flourish. For instance Ros Hutt at **Theatre Centre**, Joe Sumsion at **Action Transport** and Tony Graham at the **Unicorn Theatre** have all built companies that are there not just to put on product but to provide a living structure in which writers and theatre makers can grow. This investment in people, rather than 'product'

alone, is illustrated by Damien Cruden at **York Theatre Royal** who has joined forces with **Pilot Theatre** - giving them a creative home from which to tour. Some directors of so-called 'main house theatre' would not contemplate such a move - perhaps thinking that young people's theatre is by implication second rate.

Cruden has wiped away some of the prejudice that dogs YPT by placing **Pilot** alongside his repertory theatre, and that makes a clear statement that YPT is a real part of 'theatre Britain'.

Writers for young people and writers in general of course, need champions. At **Arts Council England** Charles Hart has been supporting writers for many years practically and artistically and will be greatly missed. I have had many such advocates in my writing career, notably Gary Meredith at **Gwent Theatre**, Phil Clark at **The Sherman**, Vicky Ireland at **Polka Theatre** and Tony Graham at the **Unicorn Theatre** to name but a few. These people, perhaps unwittingly, become the guardians of 'quality' as they engage with the writer in debates about the quality of their work. They take on the deep dramaturgical role that is an integral part of European theatre.

52

INNER BATTLES

In a more personal sense I have an army of policemen (constraints) in my head trying to stop me reaching that deep creative place where I am an artist struggling with the truth about humans. Some of these cops I've appointed myself: for instance, 'Constable, I don't want to upset people'. Well constable - get used to it. I'm a playwright - plays can be upsetting and it's sometimes very useful to upset the audience. Some of the policemen in my head are employed by the state, particularly a chief constable in the guise of the national curriculum, which forces us into bending theatre into something which ticks educational boxes - a role theatre is not well suited for though most companies are clever in playing the game.

It is not the most obvious constraints of schools; the noise of 5b going to chemistry, the bareness of the school hall (where over the years I have seen my faith in theatre reaffirmed many times) that provoke poor quality work but it's because the 'art' now needs to be seen to act upon the audience in a particular way - which makes working through metaphor difficult since the kids have to be seen to learn something in a recordable way. This means they have to be told something which remains at the top of the brain - rather than be affected by something deeply which by implication would be hard to regurgitate.

When I look at a good piece of painting or read a poem I don't ask myself, 'What do I learn from that?' So why put that pressure on my own work? Isn't it enough to really try and examine what it is to be human, now, and be true to that quest? I've seen plays by Harold Pinter mesmerise young people because of a mystery within his writing. I doubt if he ever started a work process by asking 'What are the aims of this show, how will it achieve them and what characters do we choose to deliver the themes?' This can kill the story and character long before they reach the 'empty space'.

I feel odd exploring this notion because I've become known as a writer who 'takes care of his audience', who leads them on a journey which however obscure at first, eventually becomes clear, where story is about resolution and safety. Now I'm thinking - what if they don't understand? What about not being safe in your seat? What about healthy confusion that leads to questions, and unresolved situations? Perhaps then the biggest policeman in my head is actually me, always wanting to clear up the mess of the world in a play - when it might be more useful to portray the world as it is rather than as I might wish it to be. Perhaps confusion and tragedy are more enlightening at this moment in time, than 'the well crafted tale'. Perhaps they are not mutually exclusive?

RISK

Although 'devising' with a writer is not a process I would hurriedly leap into these days, I am still very interested in finding work processes away from my desk because theatre can be made in so many ways, and the creative theatre producer can provide time and space for that to happen, for artists to 'play' and create outside of the pressure and constraints of immediate production. Artists sometimes need to be able to create without constraints and in YPT there are many - not least the children themselves. This might at first sound controversial but I only mean that the theatre we make for children is governed by the audience rather than by us as artists and maybe the balance needs to be rethought. We often ask before we create, 'will this be acceptable to them'? 'Will they understand everything in the play - will they be upset?' The chance to create without the audience directly in mind might be very releasing and productive.

I have recently been involved in two projects, which for me broke the mould. The first was *Red Red Shoes* (**Unicorn Theatre** and **The Place**) in which we explored through dance/drama the experience of ethnic cleansing in Kosova and the subsequent effect on a young girl's mental health. This play used tragedy as a stimulant and the young protagonist is killed while defending a friend. It seemed the honest way to end the story I had begun and led to much debate, among practitioners teachers and parents.

The other piece was *Playing Antarctica* (**Unicorn Theatre**) a play of a kind, without words, that told its story predominately through sound. We started from a blank sheet or really more an empty space and gradually filled it. We took the risk of losing the audience in the sense of not telling them what was happening or what the meaning was and, although not perfect by any means, I think it will stay in the minds of those who saw it longer and deeper than many other plays I've been part of with more obvious educational aims.

Charles Way

YOUNG WRITERS:
HOW THE NEXT GENERATION ARE BEING ENCOURAGED

Ben Mellor & Atiha Sen Gupta - Delegates at The Lockpickers' Ball - Photo by Sylvia Selzer

ACTION TRANSPORT:
COLLECTIVE WRITING

The Mask Session at Chester Gateway Studio – Photo by Sylvia Selzer

The Mask Session at The Lockpickers' Ball - Photo by Sylvia Selzer

Since 2004 **Action Transport** has been running collective writing projects. The company believes that, done well, this process can create great new plays and be a valuable learning tool for young and emerging writers.

In 2006 the company professionally produced *The Mask*, a play written collectively by a group of writers aged thirteen to fifty-five.

Here **Kevin Dyer**, Associate Writer with the company, reveals some key steps in the process, whilst **Louie Ingham**, Projects Manager, offers her receipe for administering such a complicated project.

'THE MASK': A PLAY BY MANY HANDS

We believe that writing is good for you. The problem is that writing plays is hard – harder than writing poems, harder than writing prose.

Ian McEwan said you have to "make a date with the desk". Good advice. But if you are a young writer, or a new writer, or a scared writer, you find that when you get to the desk, you are stuck. For those of us who believe learning is best done by doing, collective writing for theatre is a powerful, empowering tool, and a thrilling process.

In the beginning...

Evening, Friday 7th April, 2006.
The Mask began with twenty people at an open-access session in Chester Gateway Studio, with objects hung from the ceiling. A bunch of strangers, young would-be writers, came together for the very first time, and stood underneath a wellington boot, an apple, a plastic spoon, a lion mask, and dozens of other objects all suspended from the ceiling. We offered a theatrical installation experience – light, sound, sculpture – then started making up the stories of the objects. We wrote them there and then.

We read the stuff out loud. From the wellie came a story of two brothers and a muddy day in leather pumps; from a football came a story of a boy who found himself in heaven playing against George Best; and from the lion mask came the story of a young boy, obsessed with lions and safaris. All lovely material – but only one idea would last the course.

That night we made a promise – if you write the play we'll put it on. "What if it's crap?" someone asked. "We don't do crap" I said, "And anyway, if someone has a bad idea there will be someone in this room to improve it or have a better one." That is both the thesis and the quality control mechanism that drives collective writing.

The following evenings.
Writing at home. The task: to develop the idea from last week. Solitary, isolated writing – an essential part of the collective process.

Friday 28th April.
Whitby Hall, Action Transport's base.
Reading what we've got so far, starting to develop and share ideas. Having a laugh. And we quickly learnt that you had to be in the room to write the play. The ideas leapt ahead in these group sessions, and if you weren't there the whole thing went ahead without you. People soon found out that their ideas were being changed, ambushed, and developed – for the better.

Then three weeks at home.
More writing: monologues, small scenes, stuff about objects, stuff about the characters, anything. Finding out that writing your own material is liberating, thrilling, satisfying.

Saturday 27th May. Whitby Hall.
We made sculptures of the characters using objects. A professional actor did some hot seating. We started 'narrowing down', chucking ideas away. Beth pitched an idea about a girl who communicated with her dead dad by letters. Suddenly we had a character that the boy with the lion mask could meet. Two teenagers now: both interesting, off-beat. And we had a title: *Freak Club*. The professional actor raised the status of the writing, and made the things created in our heads real.

One long day in June.
Locations. The idea of the psychologist's office came as a space where Jake and Sally could meet. Some people told stories of their own visits to therapists and psychologists. Other people listened with open mouths. Sean brought in his mum who works with 'kids with problems'. We worried about Sally's story because communicating by letters with another character is a bit Jane Austen – even if the other person is dead. We argued fiercely about 'exposition' and causes for events: should we show Sally's dad hanging from the rope and his daughter finding him?

June. Bedrooms again.
To-ing and fro-ing of ideas by email. Many scenes written – all of which (apart from the first one by Claire) we would throw away. But we had a collective vision – two young people, desperate to escape their ordinary lives, into their extraordinary worlds.

July 24th - 28th.
A week's intensive development.
The composer joined us; the designer was there; three actors read and acted out scenes; writers watched, discussed, rewrote. We worked out arcs, listened to people who dropped in, but rejected their opinions, too.

We had to work fast and furious. Plays need time, thinking time, mulling and sinking-in time. We didn't have enough of that. Most importantly, we needed a scene-by-scene breakdown for...

The summer holidays..
At last... writing the play (now called *The Mask* - although the object which started it all off wasn't in it anymore. Funny that.)

The secret of collective writing, in this model, is to keep everyone in the same place. Not only the same room, but with a common understanding of character back-story, character wants, themes, plot... This allowed us to come to an agreed scene-by-scene breakdown. This was the tool that we would all take away with us. Without it, it would be impossible to scatter to the four winds over the summer break and yet all still write the same play.

End of August.
First draft finished. Many writers went back to school or away to uni, and I was working on another project. But there was still work to do, now by another dramaturg. A fresh eye was invaluable in sorting out some contradictions and repetitions that collective plays inevitably produce. We didn't give enough time to properly continue this part of the collective experiment - but it got done and it went into rehearsal. It had to; the promise to produce needed to be fulfilled.

Collective writing is a political act. It empowers because it spreads the decision making far and wide. *The Mask* allowed individuals to learn the step-by-step process of making plays. It gave them the tools to then write their own. Spurred on by collective writing young and emerging writers go on to write their own plays. True. Faye Christiansen emailed me yesterday saying she was polishing a final draft of something and it would be with me by Friday. After working on *The Leather Boy*, *Spike* and *The Mask* John Moorhouse wrote a play in the shed at the bottom of his garden, which **Action Transport** will tour professionally later this year.

The Mask was an unfinished but remarkable play. It was wrought by many hands at many different times in many different places. It was a play with a bright originality. It did not preach or teach or offer solutions. It didn't put young people at the heart of

Ben Worth in The Mask - Photo by Sylvia Selzer

the play because of any belief in empowerment or child protagonists or contact figures.

It had characters that were fresh and non-formulaic; they were not created to 'reflect' concerns, but because they were the embodiment of things going on in the writers lives'. Not once did we talk about target audiences. Never did we consider the national curriculum. But we did struggle with what we feel and think and what this girl and this boy could and would do if they met. It's a story of a boy who has retreated into some safari world who stalks a mute who communicates with her dead father by letter. It could not have been written by me or any other 'grown up' professional writer, and I don't think any company making plays for young people would have bought such a 'pitch'. The process allowed this relevant, truthful, surprising story through.

The Mask was written by:

Jessica Anderson
Harri Chambers
Faye Christiansen
Jennifer Durrans
Beth Friend
Sean Mason
Heather McGaw
Jennifer Mills
John Moorhouse
Claire Rogers
Isabelle Sowley
Crystal Stewart
Becky Woods

Ideas also came from:

Lisa Bennett
Anna Drayson
Jim Johnson
John Langford
Mark Melville
Stacey Scott
Ben Worth
Emma Lambe
Louie Ingham
Kevin Dyer
Janys Chambers

...and many others

COLLECTIVE WRITING
A SUCCESFUL RECIPE

Project Recipe:

• 1 Associate writer/professional playwright

• 12 – 15 would be writers

• 1 Project Manager/Producer

• 2 – 3 break out rooms

• 1 organisation to fully back the project

• 1 good idea

• 1 venue

• Required amount of publicity material

• Friends of the company to spread the word

Please Note! The method and ingredients will probably need adapting for different kitchens and ovens...

Preparation Time (Writing time):

~~4 months~~ 6/9 months

Cooking Time (Rehearsal time):

3 weeks in a hot studio oven

Preparation:

• Play around with good ideas for an event to hook would-be writers into, put into a box, and return to later

• Decide an accessible, creative venue

• Choose a good date and time for the writers (avoid exam time)

• Work hard to publicise the event, local press, schools, youth theatre members, writers you work with, friends of the company

On The Night:

• Create a striking visual installation that prompts the questions 'What does this have to do with writing?'

• Ask attendees to fill in their information and contact details

• Have an inspiring, challenging evening, fuelled with laughter and intrigue

• Hand out dates of the next six sessions and a development week

• Ask all attendees to email over the weekend with the Line "Yes" and then add them to the email distribution list

For The Writing Process:

• 1 laptop (with carry case for mobile work)

• 1 mobile printer

• 1 email distribution list

• ~~20~~ pens, pencils, markers *plenty!*

• 1 sheet of the team's mobile numbers

• 1 good photographer

• 3 versatile professional actors

> 1 teaspoon of energy
> Sprinkling of magic

Method:

1. Heat the initial ideas, suggestions and thoughts in a large plan, until softened

Drain any bad ideas!

2. Add the rough plot

3. Stir in the ideas for characters, bringing to the boil

4. Add the stock of a good play, including synopsis, beats, scene by scene breakdown and simmer for 1 week, until thickened

5. Add the wants and needs of the characters, find the story, season, and taste a spoonful of the mixture

6. Remove from the heat and hand over the first draft

7. Sieve any bits that are just not working, amend, delete, change, add

8. Take it out of the kitchen and hand the rehearsal draft over to the production team

9. Bake in the hot studio oven for 2 – 3 weeks, until piping hot

Serve Immediately

(preferably with an audience)

Louie Ingham

M6 THEATRE COMPANY:
MONOLOGUES

Nicola Maxfield in Weighed Down - Photo by Ian Edmondson

Carla Jo Monvid-Jenkinson - Photo by Sylvia Selzer

Over the last four years **M6 Theatre Company** has developed a successful approach to developing and touring monologues to young people in the North West. Here writer **Mary Cooper** and Artistic Producer **Dot Wood** reveal the philosophy behind the company and share some of their learning in this area.

M6 THEATRE COMPANY

The Company tours predominantly across the North West to multi-cultural audiences in areas of social and economic deprivation but also responds to demand for the work from other areas of the country. Touring to schools, early years settings, arts venues, festivals and prisons, the Company's work touches the lives of over 13,000 young people per year.

The majority of **M6's** output is specially commissioned or devised from original stories. The Company runs a vibrant participatory programme, which offers valuable opportunities for creative consultation and research with young people.

An awareness and sensitivity towards our target audience is paramount to us. Whether creating work for 3 year olds or 15 year olds, **M6's** work is guided by questions such as -

- Does the work engage with this age group?

- Will they recognise aspects of themselves, their friends, their relationships and their world?

- Does the style and imagery enhance the experience?

- Will they see things with fresh eyes?

MONOLOGUES

Alongside full-length productions, **M6** has also developed a new strand of work – a series of monologues (8 – 10 mins in length) written by a range of writers aged 16 – 60 which tour individually or as a collection. **M6's** first six monologues came from a competition mounted by the company in association with **North West Playwrights**. From 73 entries, six scripts were selected by young people for production. These toured as *Double 6*.

This growing strand of work enables the Company to perform powerful contemporary stories in the classroom or theatre setting providing young audiences with intimate, emotionally charged performances, which promote meaningful and important peer conversations.

Some of the touchstones we have developed for this work are:

• Dramatic monologues need to be just that; dramatic. They should not be prose enacted.

• We are meeting a character under pressure who, in this heightened state, is compelled to speak. They might be angry, sad, triumphant, desperate, apologetic, defensive, tempted or torn. Whatever the dominant emotion, something important is at stake. For example, in *Weighed Down* the character must make a decision about whether to accept her father's invitation to spend Christmas with him and his new family in Florida. This could risk her relationship with her mother, her sense of identity - and possibly her health. Would the visit throw her back into self destructive patterns or would it help her heal and move on? We are with her as she examines the dilemma in the light of her recent history.

• In each of the monologues, we need to sympathise with, but not necessarily approve of, the character.

• The character is on a journey, a journey in which a choice must be made or examined, a secret revealed or an uncomfortable decision justified. Whatever it is, it's a journey in which something happens. As with any play, the writer is showing this action not telling it. And as with any play, the writer should know precisely who the character is, where they are, what they want and why it's important. They should also know who the character is talking to; the audience as an audience, themselves, the new girl at school, a housing official, a best friend...

• In the short form monologues of **M6**, the action reaches a crisis, but is not resolved. This dilemna provides a springboard for a dynamic, interactive workshop, led by an experienced facilitator.

• Because the audience engage with the character as a peer and become involved and moved by their predicament, their personal investment avoids the superficial and predictable responses that young people often fall back on in workshops.

M6 plans to launch a new monologue competition in 2007 as part of the Company's 30th birthday celebrations.

Dot Wood & Mary Cooper

THEATRE CENTRE:
COLLABORATIONS BETWEEN YOUNG
APPRENTICES AND PROFESSIONAL WRITERS

Marcy Oni in God Is A DJ - Photo by Hugo Glendinning

Theatre Centre has developed an innovative approach to linking its professional touring productions with the work done by young writers. In 2006 the company produced two new linked productions - *God is a DJ*, by Oladipo Agboluaje, and *Prospero is a DJ*, by **Theatre Centre Young Apprentices**.

Here Associate Artist (Education) **Michael Judge** describes some of the processes which informed these two productions and professional writer **Noël Greig** talks about his involvement with the *Authentic Voices* programme.

THEATRE CENTRE – A BACKGROUND

Theatre Centre was founded in 1953 by Brian Way. Brian, who wrote the seminal book *Development through Drama* and was an innovator and leader seen by many as the grandfather of theatre for, by and with young people. **Theatre Centre** today is dedicated to commissioning, producing and touring the best new writing for young audiences into schools and theatres. The company builds on decades of actively supporting writers from Black, Asian and other minority backgrounds. It continues to cast productions and provide artistic leadership with reference to the cultural diversity of contemporary Britain. It nurtures the grass roots by helping teachers and mentoring teenage writers on the *Authentic Voices* scheme. **Theatre Centre** fulfils a national touring remit and makes theatre for young audiences across a range of ages and scales. It is proud to work in schools, aspiring to bring art of the highest quality into some of the most challenging yet most rewarding environments for live drama. Writers who have written for the company within the last decade under the artistic directorship of Rosamunde Hutt include Benjamin Zephaniah, Sarah Woods, Angela Turvey, Roy Williams, Noël Greig, Nasima Begum, Philip Osment, Leo Butler, Fiona Graham, Peter Rumney, Rosy Fordham, Mike Kenny and Manjinder Virk.

AUTHENTIC VOICES – YOUNG APPRENTICE WRITER PROGRAMME

In 2001, **Theatre Centre** initiated the *Authentic Voices* programme. The aim is to nurture Young Apprentice writers whose voices have not yet been heard. The young writers are given access to the same development and dramaturgical processes offered to **Theatre Centre** professional writers. The work is given readings by professional actors. In 2003, **Theatre Centre** produced *Reality Check* written by nine Young Apprentice writers, a full professional production, which toured to local schools and **Soho Theatre**. The programme has its own integrity discrete from the **Theatre Centre** commissions but provides a valuable encounter for **Theatre Centre** professional practitioners and writers. The Young Apprentices speak for young audiences and have a clear role within the company; they are young writers. As young people with an informed understanding of the process of playmaking, their thoughts and opinions are unique.

GOD IS A DJ - THE COMMISSIONING PROCESS

The process is writer - not issue-led and the writer is free to bring ideas and themes which resonate with our artistic ethos. **Theatre Centre** guides the process and will gauge the age range or type of audience at which the play will be targeted. For example, **Theatre Centre** recently commissioned Sarah Woods to write a play with a part that could be played by a learning disabled actor. Another play may be targeted at a teenage audience, another may be a family show. The process is generally writer-led and the ideas and themes come from the writer. There are, however, some instances where the process is led in the first instance by a director. This was the case with *God is a DJ*.

THE CREATIVE TEAM

Paul J Medford is an Associate Artist with **Theatre Centre**. He is an artist who combines performing with choreography and direction. Rosamunde Hutt invited Medford to develop a play, 'a musical', for the company. Medford's initial idea was based on an instrument that travelled between Africa, the United States and the United Kingdom. The object and the music would connect with different stories in the different continents. The original object was a drum which, since the play is set in 2006, became an iPod in the final script. The story structure was set up to allow for an exploration of the way dance and music travels from continent to continent. The choreography fused steps from Capoeira with Samba and West African dance. The music followed a parallel journey through Brazilian Beats, Hip Hop and a Soul Ballad. Medford and Rosamunde selected the writer Oladipo Agboluaje to work on the collaboration. The writer/director relationship grew out of meetings and emails. Medford's initial idea was moved forward by Dipo and made his own. Medford's concept of a global fusion of dance and music was given a highly political dimension, with scenes in a sweat shop in Indonesia and others in oil polluted waters off Nigeria.

GOD IS A DJ - DIARY OF EVOLUTION

2003/4
Idea germinates with **Theatre Centre** Associate Artist, Paul J Medford.

Autumn 2005
Artistic Director Rosamunde Hutt and Medford research and interview potential writers.
Writer Dipo Agboluaje offered the commission.

Spring 2006
'Think-tank' meetings between writer and director.
Designer Rosa Maggiora, Musical Director Stephen Hudson and Dramaturg Neil Grutchfield brought on board the project.

March/April/May 2006
Development workshops with *Theatre Centre Young Apprentice Writers* on the *Authentic Voices* programme. Dipo works as writing tutor with the *Young Apprentices*. A personal and political dialogue is freely exchanged. The creative energy from this dialogue fuels both Dipo's writing and that of the *Young Apprentices*.

June 2006
Try out of first draft at the **Acorn Studio, Hackney Empire**. Audience of *Young Apprentice* writers and **Theatre Centre** Professionals, Associate Artists and partners. Rigorous follow-up discussions with Base Staff at **Theatre Centre**. These discussions draw on the experience of staff watching **Theatre Centre** shows in a range of different contexts. All Base Staff are expected to have an informed input and the sense of ownership is inculcated.

This dramaturgy is summarised and disseminated to the writer and creative team in a respectful way. Dipo has several in depth meetings with Neil Grutchfield – their discussions rigorously examine plot and character.

29th August 2006
First read through of rehearsal draft.

29th August – 28th September 2006
Rehearsals

- Script develops with the input of the actors.

- Two of the actors who performed in the Try Out return for the tour.

- Specialist input for the songs, voice, choreography and Capoeira.

- Director makes major cuts to keep the running time to approximately one hour including space for the music and dance.

28th September 2006
God is a DJ opens at **Redbridge Drama Centre**

29th September 2006
First performance in a school. Swanlea School, Whitechapel, London E1.

October 2006
The Isle is Full of Noises.
Oladipo Agboluaje works in Hackney with *Young Apprentices* on the *Authentic Voices* programme.

October 21st 2006
Prospero is a DJ by *Theatre Centre Young Apprentices* performed at the **Hackney Empire Studio Theatre** alongside *God is a DJ*.

Michael Judge

Daniel Anderson in God Is A DJ - Photo by Hugo Glendinning

IMPACT OF WORKING WITH YOUNG APPRENTICES FOR THEATRE CENTRE COMMISSIONED WRITERS

The beauty and integrity of *Authentic Voices* is that its ethos is based on the full collaboration of professional artists with the young participants. Over a long period of time I worked with Michael Judge to develop the theatre-writing of a group of young people; then as co-director (again with Michael) to realise that work as a professional production - *Reality Check* - with a team of experienced actors. At all points, the writers were as involved in the process of from-page-to-production as any of **Theatre Centre's** commissioned writers. Their voices were at the heart of the work, and their involvement in the process was authentic.

Inspired by some of the stories and themes that emerged from *Reality Check*, I then went on to write a play of my own - *Trashed*. My own life and concerns were part of that play, of course; but what struck me was how my young colleagues - and by now, friends - from *Reality Check* saw how, as artists, we can collaborate on very deep levels.

That the thoughts and experiences of, for example, a young Bangladeshi woman, can impact upon those of a middle-aged, white gay man - and vice-versa.

In the 'quick-fix' world we live in - where high-profile 'community projects' can often seem to be the mechanical 'ticking of boxes' - *Authentic Voices*, with its ethos of the slow, careful development of human relationships through creative collaboration, has been one of the marking moments of my life, as a person and an artist.

Noël Greig

JENNY MILLS:
I AM A WRITER

Jenny Mills - Photo by Margaret Mills

Jenny Mills began writing for theatre as a fifteen year-old, working on one of **Action Transport Theatre Company's** collective writing projects.

Here she reflects on her journey since then, offering a valuable insight into the experiences and projects which have helped her develop her craft. She also talks personally about how it feels to be starting out and getting on as a young writer.

When Joe asked me to write on the topic of 'I Am A Writer' I eventually reached the conclusion that I had to approach it as a question – Am I, in fact, A Writer? Is that how I see myself? I think it's a very personal thing to define, but when it comes down to it, I list 'student' as my occupation.

When I was eight, however, I did call myself a writer. It's quite an embarrassing memory, because a year later I re-read the stories I'd written and realised how truly appalling they were – contrived, pretentious – really, they should have been burnt, so even though I enjoyed writing, and kept writing, I stopped thinking of myself as 'a writer'.

Three years ago I went to my first **Action Transport** session, a monologue-writing workshop at my local theatre. A year later, that single session had turned into *The Leather Boy*, a group-written play – I think there were about 80 of us at the first session, which thankfully whittled down a bit. It was my first attempt at writing for the theatre, so one of the most helpful aspects of the project was having actors involved from very early on, reading the scripts. Without this I would have had no idea what worked on stage and what didn't, so I learned how to write a scene, not a story or an essay. The project also taught me how to re-draft (and re-draft, and re-draft), helping me to discover my weaknesses – how to spot them, how to deal with them, and in some cases how to pre-empt them.

Once the script was coming together I let my pedantic nature loose, and was delighted to discover that it was actually welcomed! Because so many people had written the script there were a lot of discrepancies between the scenes, so I spent many happy hours looking through it to work on the consistency. It was a confidence boost to find that this was something that came naturally – that I had strengths as well as weaknesses.

The writers of *The Leather Boy* were encouraged to stay involved throughout the process, so I more or less lived with the company for weeks, getting a basic grounding in most areas of production - direction, lighting, acting, set design. This, again, helped me to develop as a theatre writer; it enabled me to see what information the production team need from a script, and that the creative process does not stop once the script has been written. It was also a fantastic thrill to see 'my' work come to life and it meant that there was no way I was going to let theatre writing drop.

Ben Worth and Anna Drayson in The Mask - Photo by Sylvia Selzer

Whilst working on *The Mask*, another collectively-written play, I did a lot of work on non-dialogue scenes, which wasn't something I'd looked at much before. It was difficult as a writer because the tendency is to over-narrate, to make sure that everything is verbalised and clearly explained, and letting go of that control was pretty painful, but seeing the effectiveness of the end result has definitely encouraged me to persevere with it. The other main challenge with this project was developing other people's ideas: I joined the project a short way in, which meant that I avoided the awkward 'coming up with idea' part, but meant that I had the pressure of developing themes that other people clearly felt really strongly about.

It actually made me wary of participating, but I got a real sense of achievement when I felt I'd done the original ideas justice.

One play I've written (!) that was entirely my own idea was called *You Can't Out Run a Police Car*. Usually, when I'm trying to decide what to write about, I get preoccupied with 'concepts', deciding I want to write about class inequality or something similar. This results, generally, in ideas that are far too heavy, and wouldn't be any fun to watch. So with this project I surprised myself by not over-thinking it, and trusting in the decency of my original idea, even if it was a bit bizarre. This worked out well, because the 'big' ideas developed on their own, and became nicely embedded in the play without being too pervasive.

The project involved every member of **Action Transport** writers company adopting a space in Whitby Hall, their base, and writing a play to be set in that space. I'm sure I delighted my director by choosing the props cupboard (it's not even a big props cupboard), but I'm really glad I did, because even though it was a hugely awkward space to work in it prompted me to write in what I hope was a really original and creative way, coming up with a play I would never have thought of had I been writing for a stage.

The project, for me, was a lesson in the possibilities for theatre writing, and in the importance of thinking 'inside the cupboard'.

I think that although plot development and characterisation are important, you shouldn't get so bogged down in them that you lose the passion for the project, because that's what eventually drives every play. This stood me in good stead for my most recent project with **Action Transport**, *Inspiring Landscapes*, another collaborative project (I'm getting good at these) which brought together young actors, musicians and writers from Kendal, Liverpool and Ellesmere Port. It basically meant that I was working with 20 strangers for a fortnight, and being in such an unfamiliar environment challenged me to approach the writing in a new way. The project was also unlike anything I'd ever worked on before in that most of the development came from the actors' devising rather than the writing process. As a team we all put a lot of ourselves into the play, which was pretty exhausting, and I found it difficult to detach myself from the personal aspects and look at the play objectively. So the project just flagged that up as a weakness, something that I need to look at and work on.

So if becoming a writer is such an on-going process, how can I tell when I've crossed the bridge from being a 'non-writer' to being a 'writer'? I think the answer to that is threefold. Firstly, other people's opinions are important - **Action Transport's** enthusiasm to keep me involved sometimes gives me the confidence to see myself as a writer. Secondly, I'm gradually recognising positive qualities in myself - for example, I know that my pedantic side can be useful, that I'm reliable and punctual, and that I'm enthusiastic about everything I work on. I'm less happy to proclaim my creative abilities, but I think that's coming, gradually. Thirdly, I think my biggest

moment of personal realisation came a couple of weeks ago: I was sorting through my room, getting ready for Uni, when I came across an early draft of *The Leather Boy*. As I was reading through it, scenes that I'd written two and a half years ago, I realised that my writing didn't embarrass me. And I think it was that that's given me the temporary confidence to say that yes, I Am a Writer. But it doesn't stop here, and I hope that one day I'll have the confidence, and opportunity, to list 'writer' as my occupation.

Jenny Mills

John Retallack
Director
Company Of Angels

In November 2004 I saw a Dutch version of my play *The Wild Girl* performed at the *Bronx Festival* in Brussels. It was the first time I have been an author watching his work done by another director. It prompted me to reflect how I had got to this moment in my theatre career:

> *Here is a beautifully directed play for children with the same perfectionist aesthetic that I was familiar with from growing up and competing in a theatre world whose standards in England were set – for me - by Mike Alfred's* **Shared Experience**, **Theatre de Complicite**, **Cheek by Jowl**, *Deborah Warner's* **Kick Theatre Company** *and in France and Germany by Ariane Mnouchkine, Peter Brook and Peter Stein – these were my lasting formative influences.* **ATC** *(8 years) and* **Oxford Stage Company** *(10 years) were shaped by watching the work of these companies and in meeting and sometimes knowing the directors in question. They were my 'gold standard'.*

My daughter Hanna was born in 1985 and my son Jack in 1987.

From that time I became more interested in work for children and young people. If children's books were so good, why were they not matched by a similar achievement in the performing arts? Funding was low and there was clearly no respect for this genre of work – and it showed.

POSTSCRIPT:
THE GOLD STANDARD

John Retallack - Photo by Simon Annand

All the brilliant companies that I mention above played overseas and were known in Europe – but an English company at a young people's theatre festival in Europe was a rare sighting.

They simply were not on anyone's list. The acting frustrated me – it seemed both over-energized and bored at the same time. It just seemed a place that actors really didn't want to be.

My surprise in discovering the work of **Wederzijds** and several other companies at Den Bosch was that these companies were clearly working to their own 'gold standard'. This was an 'undiscovered' theatre world as exacting and aspiring as the one that shaped me. I was – and am – an untrained theatre director and a trained teacher. The discovery of the 'perfectionist' aesthetic in the domain of theatre for young people linked worlds that I thought had no connection. The latent cultural and political significance of all this was not lost on me either – hence, for example, *Club Asylum*, *Hannah and Hanna* and David Farr's *Crime and Punishment* in Dalston, **Company of Angels'** first three productions.

That is why that Sunday in Brussels was a milestone for me. Here was a show that I had written which had been picked up by the director and company I admired most – and once again I was reminded of how much I have to learn in the playing of work for children. I had had the `gold standard' applied to my own text. They had imagined a richer and more imaginative interpretation than my own version in 2002.

Yet what inspires me and drives me forward is not the novelty of seeing a better version of *The Wild Girl* – it is the confirmation that the creation of new work for children and young people can lead to levels of theatre experience as original, luminous and poetic as in any other form of the art.

Brevity, mystery, clarity, grace – these qualities are the 'gold standard' of work in our field.

John Retallack

THE LOCKPICKERS' BALL

The Bomb post show discussion - Joe Sumsion, Jo Berry, Pat Magee and Kevin Dyer
- Photo by Sylvia Selzer

(Top to bottom) Oladipo Agboluoje and Julia Samuels; Tearlach Duncanson and Nina Hajiyianni; Charles Way - Photos by Sylvia Selzer

In February 2006 **Action Transport Theatre Company** produced *The Lockpickers' Ball* festival, in partnership with Unity Theatre, Liverpool.

We knew of many companies and writers producing fantastic plays, but what were they doing behind closed rehearsal room doors? How were they working? What was their process?

We came to the conclusion, happily, that there was no conspiracy. Creative people wanted to share their experience, they just didn't have enough time and space to do it. *The Lockpickers' Ball* provided that time and space.

"...a brilliant three days. Inspirational, thought-provoking and superbly well organised....I met some fascinating people....the festival really helped me think deeply about what I do and why I do it. I think it will have a lasting impact on my work."
Paul Whitfield, Artistic Director, Brief Candle Theatre Company

(Top to bottom) Han Duijvendak; John Doona and Anne Plenderleith; Nina Hajiyianni and John Retallack - Photos by Sylvia Selzer

An amazing job... fantastic teamwork, great attention to detail... the perfect festival!"

Jude Merrill, Artistic Producer, Travelling Light Theatre Company

"The Lockpickers' Ball was an excellent opportunity to examine, experience and explore the work of young people's theatre in a relaxed and open environment. A stimulating and enjoyable 3 days."

Sarah Lovell – Young People's Participatory Theatre Project Co-Ordinator, Arts Council England

"...the effects of this festival will ripple out through the delegates lives, and those they meet, for years to come."

Han Dujivendak, Director, Handstand Productions, Liverpool

DELEGATE LIST

Mike Akers
Education Director,
Travelling Light Theatre Company

Oladipo Agboluoje
Writer of God is a DJ,
Theatre Centre

Jess Anderson
Action Transport Writer
& co-writer of The Mask

Vicky Bell
Young People's Participatory Theatre
Youth Council Co-ordinator,
Arts Council England

Jo Berry
Speaker

Clare Boswell
Freelance Director & Workshop Leader

Chris Bridgman
Director,
North West Playwrights

Janys Chambers
Director and Dramturg of The Mask

Faye Christiansen
Action Transport Writer
& co-writer of The Mask

Guy Christiansen
Associate Artist,
Action Transport Theatre Company

Mary Cooper
Theatre Writer & co-writer /
dramaturg of Weighed Down,
M6 Theatre Company

Anne Crabtree
Board Member,
Action Transport Theatre Company

Mike Crowley
Writer,
North West Playwrights

Michael Dacks
Writer & Theatre Maker

Rowan Davies
Youth Theatre Director,
M6 Theatre Company

Sophie Davies
Support Staff,
Action Transport Theatre Company

John Doona
Writer,
North West Playwrights /
Drama Advisor,
Cheshire County Council

Han Duijvendak
Producer/ Director,
HANDSTAND Productions Ltd

Tearlach Duncanson
Drama Worker,
Live Theatre

Kevin Dyer
Associate Writer
& co-writer of The Mask,
Action Transport Theatre Company

Jess Egan
Promotions and Marketing Manager –
Action Transport Theatre Company

Bryan Elsley
Writer & Producer /
Board Member,
Action Transport Theatre Company

Vanessa Fagan
Administrator & Assistant Producer,
Company of Angels

Janna Feldman
Education Officer,
Polka Theatre

Anita Franklin
Writer,
North West Playwrights

Lyn Gardner
Theatre Critic & Speaker

Beth Goddard
Support Staff,
Action Transport Theatre Company

Robin Graham
Freelance Writer & Theatre Producer

Chris Elwell
Director,
Half Moon Young People's Theatre

Beth Friend
Action Transport Writer
& co-writer of The Mask

Bev Hancock
Action Transport Writer
& co-writer of The Mask

Nina Hajiyianni
Associate Director,
Action Transport Theatre Company

Alison Heffernan
Freelance Designer

Holly Hughes
Literary & Education Assistant,
Hampstead Theatre

Ros Hutt
Artistic Director,
Theatre Centre

Louie Ingham
Projects Manager
& co-writer of The Mask,
Action Transport Theatre Company

Charlotte Jones
Director,
Independent Theatre Council

Michael Judge
Education Associate,
Theatre Centre

Fin Kennedy
Writer of Locked In,
Half Moon Young People's Theatre

Amy Leach
Co-Artistic Director,
En Masse Theatre Company

Sarah Lovell
Young People's Participatory Theatre
Project Co-ordinator,
Arts Council England

Pat Magee
Speaker

Kathy McArdle
Artistic Producer,
Merseyside Young People's Theatre

Shelia McAnulty
Deputy Director,
North West Playwrights

Liam McCormick
Education Officer,
Royal Exchange Theatre

Julie McKiernan
Writer,
North West Playwrights

Ben Mellor
Writer & Performer

Jude Merril
Artistic Producer,
Travelling Light Theatre Company

Angela Michaels
Director of Locked In,
Half Moon Young People's Theatre

Jenny Mills
Action Transport Writer,
co-writer of The Mask / Speaker

John Moorhouse
Action Transport Writer
& co-writer of The Mask

Richard Morgan
Studio Producer,
Royal Exchange Theatre

Ben Musgrave
Literary Assistant,
Birmingham Rep Theatre

Hattie Naylor
Writer of Mother Savage,
Travelling Light Theatre Company

Helen Newall
Programme Leader;
Drama, Physical Theatre & Dance,
Edge Hill University

Michelle O'Callaghan
Youth Arts Officer,
National Museums Liverpool

Karen Parry
Finance and Premises Manager,
Action Transport Theatre Company

Matthew Pegg
Professional Theatre Writer

Sarah Philips
General Manager/ Deputy Chief Exec,
Action Transport Theare Company

Graeme Philips
Artistic Director,
Unity Theatre

Anne Plenderleith
Education Producer,
Clwyd Theatr Cymru

John Retallack
Director,
Company of Angels

Keith Saha
Co-Artistic Director,
20 Stories High

Julia Samuels
Co-Artistic Director,
20 Stories High

David Selzer
Chair of the Board,
Action Transport Theatre Company

Sylvia Selzer
Board Member / Official Photographer
Action Transport Theatre Company

Atiha Sen Gupta
Young Writer,
Hampstead Theatre

Caroline Small
Freelance Writer, Director and Performer

John Sprackland
Marketing Manager,
Southport Arts Centre

Crystal Stewart
Theatre Assistant Officer,
Arts Council England, North West /
co-writer of The Mask

Jilly Sumsion
Youth Theatre Director,
Action Transport Theatre Company

Joe Sumsion
Artistic Director/ Chief Exec,
Action Transport Theatre Company

Charles Way
Professional Writer & Speaker

Paul Whitfield
Director & Writer,
Brief Candle Theatre Company

Dot Wood
Artistic Producer,
M6 Theatre Company

89

ACTION TRANSPORT
THEATRE COMPANY

Chris Lindon in Scorcher - Photo by Cliff Brett

Action Transport is a new writing theatre company. We believe that the experiences of children and young people should be at the heart of British theatre culture.

We aim to make brilliant theatre which changes people's lives. The company acts as a 'magnet for ideas', a place for professionals and young people to achieve creative personal bests.

WE DELIVER

Productions
- exceptional theatre regionally, nationally and internationally

Research and Development
- new thinking in making theatre

Learning
- sharing our processes with others

"A timely, multi-faceted work, and an emotionally explosive piece of drama"
The Guardian on *The Bomb*

The Skeleton Key

ACTION TRANSPORT TEAM

Board of Directors
Anne Crabtree
Bryan Elsley
Brian Hallet - Vice Chair
Mike Moores
David Selzer - Chair
Sylvia Selzer

Staff
Kevin Dyer - Associate Writer
Jess Egan - Promotions and Marketing Manager
Mike Francis - Company Stage Manager
Nina Hajiyianni - Associate Director
Louie Ingham - Projects Manager
Karen Parry - Finance and Premises Manager
Jake Roney - General Manager/Deputy Chief Executive
Joe Sumsion - Artistic Director/Chief Executive

Associate Artists
Guy Christiansen
Alison Heffernan
Mark Melville
Jilly Sumsion

Awards

2003 - Meridian/Interact Award for *Dumisani's Drum*, co-produced with Vulavulani Theatre Company, South Africa

2004 - Short-listed for the arto4 Arts Council England, North West Outstanding Achievement in the Arts Award

2006 - TMA Awards Nominee: Best Actor, Paul Dodds for Ned Driscoll, *The Bomb*, October 2006

2006 - TMA Awards Nominee: Best Director, Joe Sumsion, *The Bomb*, October 2006

2006 - Winner: Writers' Guild, New Writing Encouragement Award, Joe Sumsion for *The Bomb*, October 2006

Action Transport receives regular funding from:

"The incredibly gifted Vulavulani Company of Soweto and Action Transport Theatre of the UK explode onto the beautiful Unicorn stage with enough talent, energy and charisma to fill the Albert Hall."
Emma Thompson on *Tselane's Song*

For more information on new writing initiatives and how to get involved visit:

www.thelockpickersball.info
www.finkennedy.co.uk
www.hardact.biz
www.everymanplayhouse.com
www.bbc.co.uk/writersroom
www.royalcourttheatre.com
www.channel4.com/skins
www.transmissions.org.uk
www.theatrevoice.co.uk

For more information from the contributing companies:

www.actiontransporttheatre.co.uk
www.companyofangels.co.uk
www.enmassetheatre.co.uk
www.halfmoon.org.uk
www.m6theatre.co.uk
www.theatre-centre.co.uk
www.travlight.co.uk

LINKS & RESOURCES